Christian Agenda

Chico Xavier

Christian Agenda

Dictated by the Spirit
André Luiz

Translated by Jean Annette Duncan

FEB
BUSS
British Union
of Spiritist Societies

First Edition – 08/2020

Original title in Portuguese:
AGENDA CRISTÃ
Brazil, 1948

ISBN 978-65-5570-013-8

Published by
FEDERAÇÃO ESPÍRITA BRASILEIRA
Av. L2 Norte – Q. 603 – Conjunto F (SGAN)
70830-106 – Brasília (DF) – Brazil
www.febeditora.com.br
editorial@febnet.org.br
+55 61 2101 6198

INTERNATIONAL DATA FOR CATALOGING IN PUBLICATION

L953a Luiz, Andre (Spirit)

Christian Agenda / dictated by the spirit Andre Luiz ; [received by] Francisco Candido Xavier ; [translated by Jean Annette Duncan]. – 1st edition – Brasília, DF (Brasil) : FEB, 2020.

132 p. ; 15 cm

Original title: Agenda Cristã

ISBN 978-65-5570-013-8
1. Spiritism. 2. Psychographic works. I. Xavier, Francisco Candido, 1910-2002. II. Brazilian Spiritist Federation. III. Title. IV. Series.

CDD 133.93
CDU 133. 7
CDE 00.06.02

Appreciations

The Editor of this final complete revision wishes to thank Mr S. J. Haddad, the original instigator and also the original translators, George C. Hart and Evelyn R. Morales, as well as all subsequent helpers who have contributed to the translation into English and publishing of the various editions of this very useful and instructive book.

Contents

A NOTE TO THE READER

A vast number of companions are seeking guidelines, worried about the best way to live their lives…

They would like to receive direct suggestions from the Spirit World that would elevate them to the heights of an easy victory. They would like to readjust everything that concerns their business, to all of a sudden modify the mental attitudes of their loved ones and penetrate the secrets of improvised circumstances involving the free will of others, taking advantage of the opinions of their brothers and sisters who are discarnate, inhabitants of other spheres of life. However, no one can evade the lessons of experience with their function of always instructing and perfecting.

In view of this reality, any orientation that is not based on the person's inner harmony will be nothing more than a play upon words, often laudable and beneficial, at the service of accommodation.

When people are transformed to goodness, they represent a fundamental guarantee for human happiness. That is why it is imperative, before all else, to realise the greatness of being in relation to life and the Universe, which are always touched by the Divine Wonders in their smallest details.

How can events be guided, measures adopted, manifestations controlled or brought into harmony for specific ends, if there is no equilibrium at the source of effects, situations and occurrences which lie within ourselves?

If an aborigine were to be transported into a palace of modern culture, they could not possibly demand that civilisation retrogress to the state of primitive huts to satisfy their deficiency of understanding. On the contrary, their duty would be to educate themselves in order to comprehend the progress of the world.

The astronomer whose feet are firmly planted on the ground, would not ask the stars to leave the courses set for them in infinite space by the Cosmic Laws. It is their obligation to perfect optical instruments so as to be able to reach their objectives when facing the celestial greatness.

It would be childish to keep driving away insects that swarm on an infected centre under the pretext of healing it. Logic dictates that the wound be treated and the infection removed.

Humankind, having Heaven as their inheritance, will always reflect upon Divine Paternity, in accordance to the level wherein they find themselves.

Let us, therefore, flee from the very old intentions of gaining easy access to cheap benefits.

We cannot deny the imperative need to collaborate in the journey towards evolution.

In all departments of the Universe, we will find benefactors and those who receive benefits. For the hierarchy itself to function properly it must be founded on the principles of solidarity.

Nevertheless, it would not be licit to despise favours; neither should we accustom ourselves to protection.

Systematic protection is comprehensible for the tender young plant, just as it is natural to support the beneficial vegetable that is heavily laden with produce. But for ourselves, who are affected by the revelation of immortality, we are the owners of only the most rudimentary knowledge and are far from a super production in the area of goodness. We are human spirits at some distance from our original inexperience, still lacking in virtues. We are justifiably needing to illuminate our consciences, perfect our sentiments and individual qualities, so that we do not receive God's blessings in vain.

This little course in spirituality that Andre Luiz is offering is not a presumptuous collection of rigorous recommendations. It is a friendly message to those who ask for instructions from the spiritual entities, as if the true work of salvation were resident outside of themselves. This book represents a few words from our sphere of struggle, where we learn that the miracle of perfection is the result of effort, knowledge, discipline, elevation, service and perfectioning in the temple of our "spirit".

Therefore, we are not dealing with a pretentious manual.

Here, dear Reader, you will observe only the recollection of the ancient teachings of the Master, in a new setting of words being presented for us to remember together with Him that the Divine Kingdom (the edification of God within humans) will, in truth, never come to the world through outward appearances.

*Emmanuel**
Pedro Leopoldo (MG), Brazil, 18th June 1947

* Spirit Guide of Francisco Candido Xavier

— 1 —
Christian imperatives

Learn — humbly.
Teach — practising.
Administer — by educating.
Obey — willingly.
Love — by edifying.
Fear — yourself.
Suffer — benefiting ourselves.
Speak — constructively.
Hear — without malice.
Help — by elevating others.
Assist — uplifting others.
Pass by — serving.
Pray — serenely.
Ask — with discernment.

Wait — working.
Believe — actively.
Trust — watchfully.
Receive — and distribute.
Attend — graciously.
Cooperate — with detachment.
Aid — through improvement.
Examine — with criterion.
Clarify — respectfully.
Sow — without anxiety.
Study — while perfecting.
Walk — with everyone.
Advance — helping.
Act — for the general good.
Correct — with kindness.
Forgive — always.

— 2 —
Redeeming principles

Do not forget that God is the central theme of our destinies.

Desire the well-being of others as much as you desire your own.

Reconcile quickly with your adversaries.

Respect your neighbour's opinion.

Avoid disagreeable disputes.

Lend without expecting restitution.

Give your assistance to good works happily.

Do not worry about slanderers.

Thank your enemy for the value they ascribe to you.

Help children.

Do not abandon the old and the sick.

Where benefits are concerned, think of yourself last.

Forgive with sincerity.

Criticise no one.

Repair your defects before correcting those of others.

Use faith and good judgement.

Learn how to sow, preparing a good harvest.

Do not expect grapes from the thorn bush.

Liberate yourself from the weight of excessive conventionality.

Cultivate simplicity.

Talk as little as possible about yourself and your problems.

Stimulate the noble qualities of your companions.

Work for the good of all.

Value time.

Organise your work, knowing that each day has its obligations.

Do not be anxious.

Serve everyone with detachment.

Be happy, just and grateful.

Never impose your point of view.

Remember that the world was not made only for you.

Social sciences of today present these principles as being new. However, they are ancient, having come to Earth with Christ almost twenty centuries ago. But we, who are slow to comprehend, are even slower in applying them.

— 3 —
Some christian privileges

Maintaining supreme faithfulness to God.

Forgetting personal desires when attending to Superior Design.

Humbling oneself so the hand of the Lord may be exalted.

Overcoming oneself.

Renouncing joyfully for the benefit of others.

Reaping eternal profits from temporary losses.

Working to build the Divine Kingdom.

Maintaining hope, while others despair.

Entering into the temple of silence in the midst of commotion.

Maintaining one's faith above the torment of doubts.

Silencing oneself in time to avoid hurting others.

Speaking constructively.

Listening to the Divine Friend when in solitude.

Serving without compensation.

Enduring one's own cross with valour.

Learning and profiting from one's suffering.

Loving without demanding.

Helping in secret.

Sowing with Christ, detached from the results.

Finding brothers and sisters in all places.

Cultivating the pleasure of being useful.

Discerning the just worth of causes and of things.

Purifying evil.

Assisting with sincerity those who err.

Forgiving as many times as necessary.

Overcoming obstacles.

Preserving joyfulness and sweetness.

Maintaining cheerfulness.

Detaching oneself from the deceits of the world, before the world deceives us.

Persevering on the side of goodness right to the end.

— 4 —

In your own favour

Learn to yield in favour of many, so that some will intercede on your behalf in disagreeable situations.

Help without demanding, so that others may help you without complaining.

Do not imprison others to your way of thinking; give your companion the opportunity to interpret life as freely as you do.

Be careful of the way you express yourself; gestures often speak louder than words.

Refer to yourself as little as possible; cooperate fraternally in the joys of your fellow beings.

Avoid overwhelming verbosity; the person who talks without pause tires the listener.

Leave the authorship of good ideas to others and do not worry if you are forgotten. Be convinced that any noble initiatives do not belong to you, since everything good proceeds originally from God.

Think of your adversary as a bearer of equilibrium; if we have need of friends to stimulate us, we equally need someone to show us our errors.

Be calm when arguing; your opponent's rights are the same as yours.

If you pay too much attention to the criticism of one who is inferior, then you must endure the constraints of the plane to which you have descended without feeling hurt.

Be useful everywhere, but do not attempt to please everyone; do not undertake that which even Christ still has not attained.

When faced with error, correct it first in yourself and then in others, without violence and without hate.

If treachery crosses your path, deny it the honour of indignation; examine it with a silent smile, study the process calmly and shortly afterwards, transform it into something worthy of life.

Help the envious in a fraternal manner; spite is an undisguised homage to merit, and in paying this tribute the common person torments themselves and suffers.

Within the circle of human struggles accustom yourself to serenity and strength; without these conquests it will be difficult to cease the endless repetition of inferior reincarnations.

— 5 —
Evangelical remedies

Always help.
Do not fear.
Never despair.
Learn incessantly.
Think profoundly.
Meditate more.
Speak little.
Correct, lovingly.
Work happily.
Direct, with equilibrium.
Obey, contentedly.
Do not complain.
Follow on ahead.
Observe what is beyond.

Look well ahead.
Discuss serenely.
Shed light.
Sow peace.
Spread blessings.
Struggle, elevating.
Be joyful.
Live fearlessly.
Demonstrate courage.
Display calmness.
Respect everything.
Pray confidently.
Be watchful, with benevolence.
Walk forward, progressing.
Serve today.
Await tomorrow.

— 6 —

In your benefit

Do not fret over the ignorant person; surely, they have not had the opportunities which illuminated your path.

Avoid annoyance with those who are fanatics; they remain imprisoned in exclusivism and deserve compassion just as any other prisoner.

Do not be perturbed by an ill-bred person; in most cases the one who is unsociable has a liver complaint and bad nerves.

Support the companion who is insecure; perhaps they do not have the basics, while you retain an excess.

Do not be angry with an ungrateful person; they are probably confused or inexperienced.

Help those who make mistakes; your feet walk on the same ground and even if you possess the possibility to correct them, you have no right to censure them.

Pardon the deserter; they are weak and will return to the lesson later on.

Aid the sick, thank the Divine Power for the equilibrium you are able to conserve.

Forget about your accuser; they do not know your case from its beginning.

Forgive the transgressor; life will take care of them.

— 7 —

A FRATERNAL SOLICITATION

Help with your prayers all those brothers and sisters...

who never find the time or resources to be useful to anyone;

who declare themselves affronted by ingratitude on all sides;

whose eyes are cloaked in darkness and so see evil in all situations;

who dream of a thousand castles in the clouds, but do not light one candle on the ground;

who only cooperate in the ivory tower of personal interest, unwilling to descend so as to collaborate with others;

who believe themselves to have special missions and thus entitled to exceptional benefits;

who use up precious time of listeners talking exclusively about themselves;

who give up the constant process of learning within human struggle;

who never cease to find excuses for all their faults;

who want to live like orchids in the living room of the world;

who judge themselves to be the obligatory centres of general attention;

who make a fetish of illnesses and obstacles.

These are very sick people in need of Silent Help.

— 8 —
Brothers and sisters in danger

Are those who wish to transform others, from one day to the next, by the force of mere words.

Are those who give intelligent opinions and good advice to everybody, while being heedless of their own problems.

Are those who place their minds completely in another world, without attending to the duties of the world in which they live.

Are those who are constantly concerned about defending themselves.

Are those who plan ten marvellous projects each day, without materialising even one of them in ten years.

Are those who recognise the grandeur of the Divine Truths, but never find time to cultivate them in favour of their own illumination.

Are those who continually postpone till tomorrow the task of understanding and loving others.

Are those who regard themselves exclusive proprietors of all the work in the field of charity, without ever distributing opportunities of service to others.

Are those who declare forgiveness of the offence, but who are never able to forget the injury.

Are those who find occasion to become weary of life.

— 9 —
In conversation

Do not become irritated with the person to whom you are talking if they do not meet your expectations. Perhaps you were not sufficiently clear in expressing yourself.

When addressing someone and you do not receive a prompt answer, don't complain. They are probably a stutterer; if they are not, discourtesy is a sadness in itself.

When someone does not give you the solicited information as quickly as you would like, do not become annoyed. Remember that deafness can happen to anyone.

Avoid topics that are disturbing to the listener. We all have painful periods in our life about which we need to be silent.

Refrain from asking thoughtless questions. The person who interrogates too much often offends greatly.

Cultivate courteousness with the workers of any institutions or establishments you may happen to visit. Almost always, your mind is unconcerned in such places and ignores the problems of those serving you.

Be sincere, but avoid uncharitable frankness. On the pretext of being realistic, do not try to be more honest than God, from whose Loving Authority we receive the revelations and work of each day.

If someone hurts you with an unkind response, be calm and wait. Possibly they have already politely answered others ninety-nine times, or perhaps they have just suffered some important loss.

Be helpful in your conversations. A good word always uplifts.

Remember that evil is never worth commenting upon.

— 10 —
In grave moments

Be calm. Life as a state of struggle can be good; but the state of war is never a good life.

Do not deliberate hurriedly. Circumstances, being the offspring of Superior Design, modify our experiences minute by minute.

Avoid inopportune tears. They can complicate enigmas instead of solving them.

If you have erred disastrously, do not sink into despair. Standing up again is the best measure for one who falls.

Be patient. If you cannot dominate yourself, then it is useless for you to seek understanding from someone who does not as yet comprehend you.

If the question is excessively complex, wait one more day or one more week in order to resolve it. Time does not pass in vain.

On the pretext of defending someone, do not enter into a noisy circle. There are those who make a great deal of noise merely as a matter of preference.

Be moderate in your resolutions and attitudes. In grave moments our spiritual reality is more visible.

Be careful in any kind of evaluation alluding to second and third persons. On similar occasions, others will be called upon to evaluate you.

Never proclaim your individual merits since any excellent quality is very problematical in the frame of our spiritual acquisitions. Remember that virtue is not a voice that speaks, but rather a power that radiates.

— 11 —
Preventive medicine

Think well before entering into argument. At times the debater is no more than a hot-head.

Use courage sensibly. On many occasions the courageous person is simply imprudent.

Observe your methods of cultivating the truth. Many people who presume themselves truthful are actually channels of disturbance and discouragement.

Proceed with intelligence in all situations. Do not forget, however, that many intelligent people are mere scoundrels.

Be strong in your daily struggles. Nevertheless, do not forget that many whom you think to be brave are unconsciously committing suicide.

Esteem efficiency. But do not adopt rashness on the pretext of speed.

Do not confront dangers without the resources to annul them. What we set apart as bravery is often madness.

Show valour in your attitudes. Remember, however, that valour does not consist in winning at any price, but in conquering your adversary by peaceful means.

Have courage, but be moderate in your undertakings. The distance from audacity to crime is but a few steps.

Cultivate affability and sweetness along your path. Nevertheless, do not waste your time in useless conversation.

— 12 —
Always help

When faced by night do not accuse its darkness. Learn to disperse it with light.

To condemn the swamp is useless. Help it to become purified.

Along a stony road, do not throw rocks at others. Employ the stones in useful works.

Do not condemn the clamour of others. Teach them a profitable lesson by your silence.

When faced by difficult situations, do not be swayed by uncertainty. Confront them with a clear conscience.

It is pointless to blame the thorn bush. Remove it with kindness.

Do not criticise the barren ground. Fertilise it instead.

Do not reproach the desert. Help to dig a well beneath the burning sand.

There is no advantage in disapproving when everyone else disapproves. Instead, uphold you brother or sister with a kind word.

It is always easy to observe and identify evil. However, what Christ expects from us is the discovery and cultivation of goodness, so that Divine Love may be glorified.

— 13 —
In reality

A tempest frightens. However, it will strengthen our ability to endure if we know how to receive it.

Pain lacerates. But it will perfect our hearts if we seek to profit from its passage.

Misunderstanding hurts. Nevertheless, it offers us an excellent opportunity to understand.

Struggle disturbs. However, it will be the bearer of invaluable benefits if we accept its contribution.

Desperation destroys. In the face of it, however, we find the opportunity to cultivate serenity.

Hate obscures. Still, it can unveil a blessed horizon for the revelation of love.

Misfortune overwhelms. Yet it prepares us to better console others.

Shock frightens. However, within it we can find the blessings of renewal.

Trials torment us. Nevertheless, without them learning is impossible.

An obstacle displeases. But it is a true producer of elevation and capability.

— 14 —
While...

Seek the opportunity of good deeds while you still have time. It is dangerous to keep a head full of dreams with unoccupied hands.

Kindle your lamp while there is light about your steps. No traveller can avoid the surprises of night fall.

Help those about you while you have the opportunity of doing so, because the moment will come when you will not be able to carry on without help from others.

Use your physical body to gather blessings from the Higher Life while it still works together harmoniously. The vase that held sublime essences continues to perfume the air after being abandoned.

Give your lessons wisely in the school of life while the book of trials still rests in your hands. Learning is a blessing and there are thousands of brothers and sisters nearby awaiting a scholarship in reincarnation.

Settle your accounts with your neighbour while the time is favourable. Tomorrow the entire scene could be changed.

No one should be a prophet of death, nor try to imitate the ill-omened owl. Yet while you have the opportunity to store up higher spiritual values, increase your own worth and develop treasures of the soul, knowing that your journey to another type of existence is inevitable.

— 15 —
In doing so you will profit

Comfort the despairing. You yourself will not escape the temptations of discouragement within the circles of struggle.

Lift the fallen. You do not know where your own feet will stumble.

Extend your hand to the one in need of support. Your day for receiving cooperation will arrive.

Help the sick. Your own soul is not using an invulnerable body.

Make an effort to understand the less enlightened companion. Know that you do not always have the necessary means for understanding as could be desired.

Be sympathetic towards the unfortunate. The sky will not always be sunny for you.

Be tolerant and patiently help the ignorant. Remember that there are Sublime Spirits that tolerate us and help us with heroic kindness.

Console the downhearted. You cannot foresee the surprises of your own destiny.

Help an offender with your good thoughts. They teach us how hostile and disagreeable we are when we hurt someone else.

Be kind to those dependent upon you. Do not forget that Christ himself was compelled to obey.

— 16 —
Some definitions

A benefactor is one who helps and goes on their way.

A friend is one who aids in silence.

A companion is one who cooperates without making us feel uneasy.

A reformer is one who restores himself to the ways of goodness.

A strong person is one who knows how to wait within the task of peaceful work.

An enlightened person is one who knows themselves.

A brave person is one who fears nothing in themselves.

A defender is one who cooperates without causing confusion.

An efficient person is one who acts for the benefits of all.

A winner is one who conquers themselves.

— 17 —
In truth

The saint does not condemn the sinner. They help the person without being presumptuous.

The wise person does not ridicule one who is ignorant. They instruct them in a fraternal manner.

The enlightened person does not insult those walking in darkness. They illuminate their pathway.

The instructor does not blame the stumbling apprentice. It is the insecure sheep which most needs the shepherd.

The good person does not persecute one who is bad. They assist them to better themselves.

The strong person does not malign the weak. They help them to raise themselves up.

The humble person does not avoid one who is proud. They cooperate silently in their favour.

The sincere person does not disturb others. They bring harmony to all.

The unpretentious person does not criticise the vain. Whenever necessary they help them without ostentation.

The Christian person does not hate or hurt. They follow Christ, serving the world.

Otherwise, titles of virtue would only be external coverings which time would destroy.

— 18 —
Useful reminders

Do not continually ask for spiritual guidance. If you already possess two weeks' worth of Christian concepts, then you understand enough to know what to do.

Do not waste your energy trying to straighten out others by imposition. When we straighten ourselves out we will realise that the world is administered by Divine Wisdom and that the obligation to cooperate continuously towards goodness is our fundamental duty.

Do not blame the suffering discarnate spirits for your failures in life's struggles. Note the rhythm of your own life, examine your income and expenditures, your actions and reactions, your manners and attitudes, your obligations and decisions and you will recognise that you have the situation you sought and that you reap exactly what you have sown.

Do not appeal systematically to your spiritual friends with regard to petty, everyday tasks. They are equally busy and confront problems greater that yours and their responsibilities are more grave and immediate. Within the common struggles on Earth, you would not have the courage to ask a generous and kind professor to perform the functions of a baby sitter.

Do not wait for death to solve the problems of life, nor claim sickness or old age as an excuse to stop learning, because we are still very far from Heaven. The grave does not bring a miraculous transformation, but it opens a wider door of access to our own conscience.

— 19 —
A MATTER OF CHOICE

Look for a delinquent and you will find many offenders. It is necessary, then, for you to possess an immense reserve of love in order to reform them without becoming criminal yourself.

Seek to identify a fault and you will find innumerable ones. Faced with this situation, it is essential that you be sufficiently enlightened so as to not add your errors to the errors of others.

Try to locate one thorn and you will encounter various thorn bushes. In such a case, it is necessary that you remain very well balanced in order not to hurt yourself.

Place too much attention upon a stone in the road and, shortly, the ground will become very stony to your eyes. After that, you will need a great deal of resistance not to succumb to the roughness of the journey.

Approach goodness, look for it with determination and kindness will illuminate you path. Only then will you be perfectly equipped to win the war against evil.

— 20 —
Natural conclusions

The patient person never despairs.

The anxious person sooner or later complains.

The brave person endures difficulties by overcoming them.

The reckless person confronts danger without ponderation.

The enlightened person stands out.

The theorist talks excessively.

The friend studies ways to help.

The adversary watches for means to hurt.

The common person helps according to their inclinations.

The Christian will always help.

— 21 —
Sowing

Your generosity will call the goodness of others to your aid.

Your simplicity will solve problems for many people.

Your complexity will give rise to much insincerity in others.

Your indifference will produce visible coldness in others.

Your sincere desire for peace will guarantee tranquillity along your path.

Your belligerency will bring forth fruits of anxiety.

Your blunt frankness will provoke rough responses.

Your refinement will inspire correct manners in those who follow you.

Your superior spirituality will motivate sublime spiritual achievements.

We sow and we reap daily. Life is also a soil which receives and produces eternally.

— 22 —
Even further

To have a mouth that is perfumed is not enough. It is imperative that it be incapable of hurting others.

The cleanliness of your hands is important. However, it is essential to verify what they do.

Good ears are certainly a treasure. However, Divine Justice will want to know what you are listening to.

Excellent vision is a laudable quality. Nevertheless, it is of interest to note how you look at life.

To have physical health is to possess a valuable gift. But it is necessary to consider what you do with your healthy body.

Clear reasoning is a virtue. Still, it is essential to observe in what mental zone you are reasoning.

A beautiful imagination is like having a marvellous castle. However, it is well to note with what images you furnish your inner palace.

Strong emotions characterise internal richness. Nevertheless, it is necessary to verify how you spend your emotions.

The ability to be intensely productive is a precious resource. But it is essential that you know the substance of that which you produce.

The capacity to proceed joyfully through life is a blessing. Nevertheless, remember to watch the direction your feet are taking along the way.

— 23 —
Realities

The clown that you mock is frequently a brave soldier of good cheer.

The extremely adorned woman of whom you usually disapprove, is on many occasions dressing like that in order to help a great number of working hands.

The singer who performs smiling, from whom you often turn away in boredom, in the belief that you are preserving your own virtue, is usually trying to earn bread for many needy relatives and thus deserves consideration and respect.

A well-to-do person who appears to you to be lazy and unproductive is perhaps involved in projects that you would never find the animation to tackle.

Do not judge others by their appearance. The truth, like the Kingdom of God, is never displayed in outward appearances.

— 24 —
Appearances

Do not accuse the person who appears to be wealthier. Perhaps they are merely a slave to obligations.

Do not condemn the companion who was raised to a position of authority. He is probably a mere debtor to the multitude.

Do not envy the one who administers while you obey. Frequently they are suffering a painful process.

Do not disdain the colleague who is conducted to greater prominence. The responsibility which weighs on their shoulders can be an incessant torment.

Do not censure the woman who dresses luxuriously. For her, luxury is probably a bitter trial.

Do not criticise the polite in manner who seem insincere at first sight. Possibly they are avoiding enormous crimes or great disappointments.

Do not fret over the ill-humoured friend. You do not know all of their inner difficulties.

Do not become displeased with the person whose conversation is futile. You were also like that when you lacked experience.

Do not mutter against the inconsiderate young. Help them whenever you can, remembering that you were once considered to be irresponsible by many people.

Do not be intolerant in any situation. The clock ticks incessantly and you will likewise face numerous difficult problems along your own path as well as on the paths of those you love.

— 25 —
Ascend higher

Do not be hurt by slander. Live in such a way that no one will believe the slanderer.

Do not be set back by perturbations. Follow your path attending to the superior purposes of life because the makers of confusion will be many.

Do not be concerned with unwarranted accusations. You can realise many valuable plans to counteract the unjust accusers.

Do not be troubled by untoward mistrust. You can employ your clear conscience in honest service anywhere.

Do not become discouraged by criticism. Censure is something within everyone's reach, but elevated achievements are the work of only a few.

Do not become disheartened by unfavourable opinions. If you remain devoted to goodness, the approval of your own conscience will prevail over any opinion, no matter how respectable.

— 26 —

If you so desire

If you desire to become in effect a Christian, then:

by losing, you will win in the human battle;

by yielding, you will obtain the resources you need;

by working, you will attain your own happiness;

by forgiving, you will edify those around you;

by liberating, you will conquest others;

by enduring, you will withstand the storm;

by renouncing, you will gain immortal treasures;

by blessing, you will save many;

by suffering, you will receive more light;

by sacrificing yourself, you will find peace;

by hard work, you will purify yourself;
by loving, you will always illuminate.

— 27 —
Difficult experiences

Physical beauty can bring about unforeseeable tragedies for the soul that lacks discernment.

Excessive money is a door to pauperism, if the one who possesses it cannot maintain their own balance.

Too much comfort is a disadvantage, if one does not learn the art of detaching oneself from it.

Prominence can be an introduction to a spectacular fall, of one does not mature one's reasoning.

Too great an authority spoils the joy of living, if the mind does not cultivate a sense of proportions.

Too heavy a responsibility can exterminate the existence of one who has, as yet, not risen above ordinary understanding.

An enormous amount of knowledge in the midst of many ignorant, vulgar or foolish people is a poisonous and bitter fruit, if the spirit has not yet become resigned to solitude.

— 28 —
Effectively

To be vigilant does not mean distrust. It means enlightening yourself by means of helping those who find themselves in the shadows.

To defend is not a matter of shouting. It is to render more intense service to causes and to people.

To help is not to impose. It is to give substantial support, without craving for personal recognition, so that the beneficiary may grow, become enlightened and find happiness of their own accord.

To teach is not to hurt others. It is to lovingly guide them towards the kingdom of understanding and peace.

To renovate is not to destroy. It is to respect the foundations and so restore the works for the general good.

To enlighten is not to argue. It is to assist, through a spirit of service and good will, the understanding of those who lack knowledge.

To love is not to desire. It is to always be understanding, give of oneself, renounce one's own whims and sacrifice oneself so that the Divine Light of true love may shine forth.

— 29 —
It is reasonable to think on this

Patience is not a colourful stained-glass window for you to enjoy in your leisure hours. It is added help when facing obstacles.

Serenity is not a garden to be cultivated for your cheerful days. It is a provision of peace for the deceptions along your path.

Calmness is not a harmonious violin to accompany your pleasant conversations. It is a substantial asset against possible misunderstandings.

Tolerance is not a delicious wine to be enjoyed in your moments of fellowship. It is a valuable door through which you may demonstrate good will to your less advanced companions.

Real co-operation is not just the easy process of receiving assistance from others. It is a means of helping a friend in need.

Confidence is not a nectar to sweeten your moonlit nights. It is a secure refuge for tempestuous hours.

Optimism does not constitute ease for your twilight hours. It is a source of power for difficult days.

Fortitude is not a rhetorical ornament. It is a reinforcement to your faith.

Hope is not the act of kneeling for simple contemplation. It is energy for the lofty realisations that belong to your spirit.

Virtue is not a decorative flower. It is the blessed fruit of your own effort which you should use and glorify in the appropriate moment.

— 30 —
Replies to those in haste

Avoid impatience. You have already lived countless centuries and are now standing before endless millenniums.

Keep calm. But flee from idleness as one who recognises the decisive value of each minute.

Spread love. Think of the devotion of the One Who has loved us from the beginning.

Keep your balance. Unbridled passions and desires are forces of destruction within the Divine Creation.

Cultivate confidence. Tomorrow the sun will reappear on the horizon and the landscape will be different.

Intensify our own efforts. Your life will be what you make of it.

Cherish solidarity. You will not be able to live without others, although in the majority of cases others can live without you.

Experience solitude from time to time. Jesus was alone in the crucial moments of His passage on Earth.

Give constructive action to your hours. However, do not convert your existence into a Tower of Babel.

Render your faithful devotion to peace. But remember that you will never experience tranquillity without giving peace to those who cross your path.

— 31 —
Reveal yourself

In your daily struggles, do not demand politeness from your companion. Demonstrate yours.

Referring to good deeds, do not wait for collaboration. Before all else, be the first to collaborate.

In trivial tasks, do not demand the effort of others. Show your own good will.

In jobs that require understanding, do not ask your neighbour to rise to your level. Learn to descend to theirs and help them.

When performing Christian duties, do not wait for outside resources to fulfil them. The best thing that you can give to good works is your own heart.

In the ordinary dealings of life, do not wait for others to reveal their excellent qualities. Express the elevated gifts that you already possess.

In every earthly creature there exists light and shadow. Allow your own goodness to become conspicuous so that the goodness of others may come to join you.

— 32 —
Signs

Your conversation indicates the directions you have chosen in life.

Your decision, taken in grave moments, identify the true position of your spirit.

Your attitudes, within daily struggles, speak of your inner climate.

Your impulses define the mental zone in which you prefer to operate.

Your thoughts reveal the kind of spiritual companions you keep.

Your reading habits define your sentiments.

Your personal treatment of others demonstrates the point to which you have progressed.

Your requests shed light upon your objectives.

Your opinions reveal the true place which you occupy in the world.

Your days are marks along the pathway of evolution. Do not forget that great assemblies of companions, both incarnate and discarnate, know your personality and follow you along your pathway by the signs you leave behind.

— 33 —
Without these resources

Without good manners, you will be deprived of the confidence of others.

Without fortitude, you will succumb to the first obstacles on your path.

Without positive faith, you will wander aimlessly.

Without devoting yourself to goodness, you will experience a terrible inner hardening.

Without giving noble examples, you will pass uselessly through the world.

Without dignified work, tedium will corrode your energies.

Without personal effort, you will never reach the doors to Higher Planes.

Without hope, your earthly nights will be even darker.

Without comprehension, your journey through the shadows will be painful.

Without a spirit of renunciation, you will not be able to educate anyone.

— 34 —
Be prepared

Balance your sense of justice, subtracting from it your inclination towards vengeance.

Be on guard against your fearlessness, lest is become an act of recklessness.

Analyse your firmness, so that it will not be transformed into petrification.

Illumine your directives, so they will not be converted into tyranny.

Examine your cleverness, so avoiding your internment within villainy.

Take care that suffering does not become revolt.

Control your resentments, to avoid installing them in the sinister house of hatred.

Keep watch over your frankness, so that your words will not distil poison.

Watch over your enthusiasm, so that it will not constitute thoughtlessness.

Cultivate your noble zeal, but do not turn it into a dark primer of violence.

— 35 —
Learn with nature

The sun shines from on high, in order to help everyone.

The stars group themselves in order.

The sky has its timetable for hours of light and of darkness.

Although it continues to be linked to the soil, the vegetable abandons the dark hole in search of light so it may produce.

The bough that survives the storm yields to its passage, nevertheless it continues to maintain its appropriate place.

The rock guarantees the life of the valley, by resigning itself to solitude.

The river reaches its objectives because it has learned to flow around obstacles.

The bridge serves the public without making exceptions, by asserting itself against extremism.

The vase is useful to the potter, after enduring the heat of the kiln.

The gem shines, after submitting to the files of the stonecutter.

The canal is able to fulfil its finalities, because it does not lose access to the reservoir.

The harvest always yields in accordance with the purposes of the sower.

— 36 —
Logically

The person who feeds on hatred pours fire into their own heart.

The person who upholds vice becomes its prisoner.

The person who cultivates idleness surrounds themselves with a wall of ice.

The person who becomes angry is the inquisitor of their own soul.

The person who delights in criticism casts stones upon themselves.

The person who provokes difficult situations increases the number of obstacles they face.

The person who judges hastily is always analysed with haste.

The person who specialises in identifying evil will find it difficult to see goodness.

The person who does not wish to endure is incapable of serving.

The person who lives collecting lamentations will walk under a shower of tears.

— 37 —
Liberate your soul

Do not become attached to the beauty of ephemeral forms. The flower lasts but briefly.

Do not heap up precious things that weigh in the scale of the world. Golden chains can bind as much as bronze handcuffs.

Do not become a slave to opinions of the frivolous and ignorant. *Incitatus*, Caligula's horse, ate from a bucket adorned with pearls, still it did not stop from being a horse.

Do not nourish the greed for possessions. The coin collector's house is full of coins which served millions, but whose owners have disappeared.

Do not give up your constructive freedom because of human opinions. The trap that punishes the ferocious animal is the same that surprises the negligent canary.

Do not believe in the flattery which lends you imaginary qualities. Cruel wasps frequently hide themselves in the calyx of the lily.

Do not worry about acquiring immediate benefits in the Earth experience. Museums remain crammed full of cloaks of kings and other "cadavers of dead advantages".

— 38 —

Do not ruin your day

Your irritation will not solve any problems.

Your contrarieties will not alter the nature of things.

Your disappointments will not do the work that only time will achieve.

Your bad mood will not modify life.

Your pain will not stop the sun from shining tomorrow over the good and the bad.

Your sadness will not illuminate pathways.

Your lack of enthusiasm will not edify anyone.

Your tears will not replace the sweat and effort which you ought to employ for the benefit of you own happiness.

Your complaints, even if affectionately construed, will never increase other's sympathy for you by one ounce.

Do not ruin your day. Learn from Divine Wisdom to forgive endlessly, always constructing and reconstructing for the Infinite Good.

— 39 —
WITH JESUS

Renunciation will be a privilege for you.

Suffering will glorify your life.

Tests will expand your powers.

Work will be as a mark of confidence along your pathway.

Sacrifice will sublimate your impulses.

Bodily illness will be a beneficial remedy for your soul.

Slander will honour your task.

Persecution will be a motive for you to bless many.

Anguish will purify your hopes.

Evil will summon your spirit to the practice of good.

Hate will challenge your heart to manifestations of love.

The Earth, with all its contrasts and unceasing renewals, represents a blessed school of individual perfection in whose purifying lessons you will leave selfishness crushed forever.

— 40 —

You can be sure...

You can talk about kindness at every moment, but if you are not kind, it will be useless for your own happiness.

Your hand can write beautiful pages under spiritual inspirations; however, if you do not stamp the beauty of those pages onto your spirit, you will not be more than a courier without intelligence.

You can read marvellous books with emotions and tears; still, if you do not apply what you have read you will only be a bad recorder.

You can cultivate sincere convictions in matters of faith; nevertheless, if these convictions do not serve to renew you for the good, your mind will be reduced to a mere hook whereon to hang religious maxims.

Your capacity to offer guidance can discipline many people, so improving their personalities. Still, if you do not discipline yourself, the Law will face you with the same severity with which it utilised you to perfect others.

You may know the lessons of the pathway perfectly and may, in the mortal eyes of the world, pass to the gallery of heroes and saints; but if you do not practise the good teachings you know, the Divine Laws will determinate that you always have to begin your work over again, each time with greater difficulty.

You may call Jesus: "Master" and "Lord"; however, if you do not want to learn to serve with Him, your words will sound hollow, without meaning.

— 41 —
Defend yourself

Do not turn your ears into a storehouse of rumours.

Intrigue is a viper that will lodge in your soul.

Do not transform your eyes into lenses of vilification.

The images that you corrupt will remain corrupted on the screen of your mind.

Do not turn your hands into spears in order to fight without profit.

Use them in the field of goodness.

Do not underrate your creative faculties by focusing them on easy pleasures. You will answer for what you did with them.

Do not condemn your imagination to permanent excitation.

Your inferior creation will torment your inner world.

Do not lead your feelings towards a lust for suffering.

Teach them to delight in the enjoyment of service to humankind.

Do not search for the pathway to paradise, while directing others towards the road to hell. The way to heaven will be built within yourself.

— 42 —
You, yourself

Remind yourself that you are:

- the best secretary for your tasks,

- the most efficient publicity agent of your ideas,

- the clearest demonstrator of your principles,

- the highest standard of the lofty teaching your spirit embraces

- and the living message of the noble ideas that you transmit to others.

Equally, do not forget that:

- the greatest enemy of your most noble realisations,

- the complete or incomplete negation of the sublime idealism that you proclaim,

- the discordant note of the symphony of goodness that you intend to execute,
- the architect of your afflictions
- and the destroyer of your opportunities for elevation - is you, yourself.

— 43 —
Personal problems

Living faith is not a transferable property. It is a personal conquest.

Legitimate happiness is not merchandise that can be borrowed. It is an inner realisation.

Grace does not descend from heaven at random. It has to be earned.

The best charity is not that which is done by substitutes. We must perform it ourselves.

Moral strength is not the result of others pleading for us. It comes from our own effort to take a stand on the side of goodness.

Steadfast hope does not dwell firmly in our hearts by mere contagion. It is the offspring of higher understanding.

Real love is not born from the shadows of desire. It is a crystalline and inexhaustible fountain of the eternal spirit.

True knowledge is not the achievement of but a few days. It is the work of time.

Paradise will never be acquired by astute bargaining. It is attainable through our good will in avoiding the purgatory or hell of our own conscience.

The protection of the Higher Planes is an unquestionable fact for all of us who still move within the shadows. Woe to us, however, if we do not seek the blessings of enlightment.

— 44 —
Rise above

When looking at a block of crude stone, do not dwell on its possible weight. Remember the perfect statue that will emerge from it.

When contemplating the difficulties of sowing, do not let the fears of torrential storm or blight detain you. Think of the grain that will overflow in the granary.

When facing a storm, do not loose yourself in lamentations. Meditate upon the benefits that its passage will bring.

When faced with hard work, do not be afraid of the copious sweat it will produce. Centralise your expectations on the good that will result from it.

Do not be preoccupied with the heat of the forge. Look towards the useful articles with which it will furnish your life.

Do not picture only the dangers of illness. Reflect upon the joy and the possibility of being able to cure.

If you are governed effectively by a higher ideal, forget the friend who deserted, the wife who fled, the ungrateful companion or the difficult relative. All of them are learning and passing by, just as you are... What matters is the intensification of the light, the progress of truth, and the victory of goodness.

— 45 —
Always called

Christians are called to serve everywhere.

In a house of suffering, they will administer consolation.

In the den of ignorance they will offer enlightenment.

In a castle of pleasure they will teach moderation.

On the brink of criminality they will impede the fall.

In an ambient of drunken abuse they will exemplify sobriety.

In dark hideaways, they will kindle light.

In the fog of despondency they will open the doors of encouragement.

In the inferno of hatred they will multiply the blessings of love.

In the market-place of malice they will distributes goodness.

In the courts of justice they will put themselves in the place of the accused, so they may examine the errors of others.

At every turn of the path we encounter suggestions from the Lord, challenging us to serve.

— 46 —
SEIZE THE OPPORTUNITY

It is not the docile companion who most needs your immediate fraternal understanding. But the one who still struggles to subdue the ferocity of the wrath which lies within their breast.

It is not the person who is full of evangelical understanding that requires your most urgent attention. But the one who still has not succeeded in eliminating the viper of malice from within their heart.

It is not the friend marching peacefully along the path of goodness who insistently solicits your care. But the one who is lost in the thicket of discord and misunderstanding, who is without strength to return to the straight path.

It is not the person who goes about their normal work that requires urgent help. But the one who did not have sufficient resources to conquer the constraining circumstances of human experience and so fell into the dark zones of derangement.

It is very probable that, for the time being, your cooperation in paradise is completely dispensable. However, the unquestionable reality for the moment is that your place of service, learning, helping and loving is right here on Earth.

— 47 —
Entreaties

In prayer you ask for a ray of Light, but almost always you forget that you have at your disposal the solar focus point to help you fulfil the Sublime Objectives.

Your spirit supplicates a glimmer of love, while all around you Humanity awaits the manifestation of your capacity to love.

You beg for the concession of favours that enable you to collaborate with Divine Wisdom, forgetting that millions of beings are waiting for your willingness to serve, in the name of the Heavenly Father.

Your heart demands heavenly signs, and, while the Wisest of the Wise colours the flowers and the horizons for your eyes to see, you search for vain diversions and notice nothing.

You demand justice for your personal affairs and daily complicate situations and problems, without ever noticing that Supreme Harmony always rectifies everything around you, through the intermediary of pain and death.

You desire opportunities for growth and ascension to higher spirituality, but frequently run away from the various degrees of laborious and humble work offered to you daily, conceded by the One Who is Infinitely Good, in the name of mercy.

If you are always entreating eternal happiness, yet refusing the resources enabling you to acquire it, what can you expect?

— 40 —
CONSULTING GOODNESS

The slanderer wants you to see the ugliness they see in the lives of others.

The weak and hesitant person expects your strength to be brittle.

The contentious person will await your presence to take part in disputes against everybody and everything.

The ungrateful person will not be happy at seeing you being recognised by others.

The egotistical person does not rejoice at seeing your respect for adversaries.

The revolted person will attempt to fix a mask of rebellion to your face.

The confused person will try to plunge your mind into the depths of turmoil.

The neurasthenic will ask you not to smile.

The foolish person will demand your adherence to madness.

The person who is as yet imperfectly spiritualized, always seeks to liken their fellow creatures to themselves. Nevertheless, remember that you are yourself, with an original task and different responsibilities and if you aim at real happiness you should never forget to consult the patterns for goodness, together with Christ, at every moment of your life.

— 49 —
HELP YOURSELF

Covet nothing belonging to your neighbour unless it be the excellent qualities that adorn their spirit.

Do not let annoyances govern the helm of your destiny.

Do not deliver the temple of your memory to evil impressions.

Do not detract the spiritual aspects from your experiences.

Do not forget that the higher ideal, which is the object of your admiration, should become manifest along your pathway.

Do not be enslaved by evil; meanwhile, do not shun the obligations of fraternity towards those who have been attacked by evil.

Do not put out the torch of faith during days of brightness, so as not to be deprived of light during the dark ones.

Do not run away from the lessons to be learnt along your evolutionary path, however difficult or painful they may be, so that later on life may open up its sanctuary of wisdom to you.

Do not neglect to find the time to cultivate what is beautiful, eternal and good.

Do not forget that justice establishes universal order, but that it is only love which expands the work of God.

— 50 —
Conclusions

That physical life is a blessed school, is unmistakable. But, if you do not take advantage of it so as to sufficiently learn the lessons intended for your spiritual growth, then your entrance into human apprenticeship will be worth nothing.

That the path of goodness is laborious and difficult is undeniable. However, if you are not disposed to follow it, then no one will free you from the dangerous influence of evil.

That eternal happiness is a supreme achievement, way beyond the transient state in the flesh, is indisputable. Nevertheless, if you desire to continue in the field of easy and inferior pleasures of the lowest levels, then you will wander in them indefinitely.

That God is with us in all circumstances, is an unquestionable truth. Still, if you are not with God, no one can foresee to what depths your spirit will descend in the domains of intranquillity and darkness.

About The Medium

The well-respected Brazilian medium Francisco Candido Xavier received Christian Agenda through automatic writing.

In order to more fully appreciate the contents of this book, a few words should be said about this remarkable, but humble man. Though his education did not go beyond the four years schooling of the rural elementary system of his country, he nevertheless, wrote over four hundred books dictated by Evolved Spirit Messengers.

All through his sixty years of voluntary service, he helped thousands of people through the amazing letters received by automatic writing from departed relatives and family members bringing consolation and confirmation as to survival after the so-called death. He also spent many hours comforting and advising people towards finding a better way of life. For this intensive work and the patient ear he used to lend to people's problems, he never received any payment whatsoever. The copyrights of all his books were donated to help the poor and the Spiritist movement in general, because these books, being mediumistically received, did not belong to him.

Assisted by highly Evolved Spiritual Guides, "Chico" as everybody called him, constantly sought to regulate his life to be in accordance with these lofty standards. Those who came to know him bore witness to this fact on many occasions. His attitude towards mediumship and service may be summed up as faithfully reflecting the injunction of Jesus made to His Disciples, to give for free what they had received for free.

Publishing Committee:
Jorge Godinho Barreto Nery – President
Geraldo Campetti Sobrinho – Publishing Coordinator
Cirne Ferreira de Araújo
Evandro Noleto Bezerra
Maria de Lourdes Pereira de Oliveira
Marta Antunes de Oliveira de Moura
Miriam Lúcia Herrera Masotti Dusi

Publishing Producer:
Fernando César Quaglia

Translated by:
Jean Annette Duncan

Cover:
Evelyn Yuri Furuta

Graphic Design and Layout:
Luciano Carneiro Holanda

Technical Standardization:
Library of Rare Works and Book's Patrimonial Documents